Hospitality Event Planning Handbook
By
Robert Villegas

Hospitality Event Planning Handbook
By Robert Villegas

©Copyright 2015 Robert Villegas, Jr.

Published in the United States of America by
Document Services International

info@documentservicesinternational.com

www.documentservicesinternational.com

Table of Contents

Introduction

Your boss has just told you that he wants you to manage a hospitality event for your company's top clients. The event will be held in conjunction with a sporting event in a major league sport.

How will you do it? You may not know how to start, what to do and how to ensure that the event is successful. After you pick your stomach off of the floor, you say, "Ok" and begin to leave his office. Then he says, "Here, use this." He has just handed you a copy of the "Hospitality Event Planning Handbook" and suddenly the world is a normal place again.

This handbook is a result of years of experience in holding hospitality events in a number of different formats. It will provide you with all of the time-tested tools you will need to create the event management team, determine what needs to be done, who will do it, how they will do it and when. Sample documents and worksheets make planning and implementing your event easy and stress free.

Getting Started

Corporate hospitality provides your company with an opportunity to achieve some basic business goals in a casual setting. The better you understand the opportunity and how to conduct a good hospitality event, the better you can maximize your results. Nothing happens without a plan and nothing good happens without a good plan.

You can use a corporate hospitality event to meet one or more of the following goals:

- o Thank your best customers for their loyalty and business
- o Attract new customers – get the signature on the contract
- o Build relationships between your sales and management employees and your customers
- o Create shared memories and experiences that create a positive image of your company in the minds of your customers
- o Have fun with your customers.

The first thing you want to do is set your benchmark for the event. You want to find something measurable that you can use to later compare against so you can brag to your boss about how successful your event was and how much your raise should be and how much of a promotion you deserve. Normally, it is good to develop three forms of benchmark.

1) Overall business from the entire customer base
2) Overall business from the customers to be invited
3) A budget of projected and (later) actual costs of the event
4) If this is an annual event, see if you can get any similar numbers for past years.

Set up a folder or document with this information so that you can later use it for your event final report.

The next step is to talk with your boss about his expectations and the deliverables. Discuss specific logistical issues that concern him and the bottom line results in terms of results. If he wants to see an increase in business from the invited customers ask him what he would consider a reasonable expectation compared to companies not invited. Ask him if he has any particular clients that he'd like to see invited and any preferences on the team that he'd like to see pull it off. Finally, ask him which key individuals he thinks should be your second or backup for this activity. This person will be your "go fer" someone that will assist you with ensuring things go well and to plan.

Once you've gotten your bosses input and expectations, you will want to create a marketing plan that you will use to guide your decisions during the coming weeks. Below is a sample marketing plan to give you an indication of issues to cover.

The Integrated Marketing Program Sample

Business to Business Hospitality Program

Objectives: Maximize relationships with businesses to promote larger sales and long-term relationships. Enjoy a relaxing day with our top customers
Audience: To 200 customers.
Timing: In conjunction with Indianapolis 500 Practice activities.
Tools/media: Hospitality tent, top sales executives, racing personality, outdoors enjoyment of practice activities at Indianapolis Motor Speedway.
Goals: To become more familiar with our top customers. To gain at least 25% increase in new business from top customers.
Measurement: Comparison of previous three months business activity with post three months activity from these clients and comparison of total client base previous three months activity with invited guest three months post-event activity

MANAGING HOSPITALITY

Managing hospitality at an event requires careful planning and execution – especially teamwork. Each event should have a thorough and well executed hospitality planning calendar. A planning meeting should be held determine necessary actions and who will execute them. The following is provided as an aid in this planning. This can be done using the tables in this document or a project planning software program like Microsoft Project.

Getting Started

This manual is designed to assist the corporate hospitality team in ensuring that all customer appreciation activities take place with a minimum of complication and maximum efficiency. The Team Coordinator and Field Coordinator are responsible for seeing to it that that activities move along without difficulty and that all fixes are made before they become problems.

Customer Appreciation Implementation Team:

The Implementation Team consists of a Team Coordinator and a Field Coordinator. These two individuals are responsible for ensuring that all other team members are aware of their responsibilities and know when those responsibilities must be completed.

TEAM COORDINATOR
A. Qualifications
1. Must be a current Manager/Supervisor with Senior Account responsibility at the minimum and Sales Manager supervisor responsibility at the maximum. Must have top level management responsibility so as to ensure cooperation with top level management in terms of ensuring that all team members' other job responsibilities can be adjusted to the requirements of the Customer Appreciation Implementation project.

B. Responsibilities

The District Team Coordinator is responsible for the successful completion of all activities for the project. With the assistance of the Field Coordinator, he should follow the progress of all scheduled activities and ensure that they occur in a timely fashion, make decisions about any activities not completed on time and make other adjustments as necessary.

This assignment includes the training of all Team Members, Supervisors and Assistants. The Team Coordinator monitors the scheduling and completion of all activities listed on the Weekly Implementation Calendar.

FIELD COORDINATOR

A.   Qualifications

Must be a current Manager/Supervisor with Senior Account responsibility.

The Field Coordinator is responsible, along with the District Team Coordinator, for the successful completion of all activities for the project. The Field Coordinator will take direction from the District Team Coordinator in visiting, communicating and otherwise ensuring that all activities in the field are moving forward as envisioned by the District Team Coordinator.

THE WEEKLY IMPLEMENTATION CALENDAR

The Weekly Implementation Calendar is designed in two parts. The Calendar has an explanation of each activity and a Weekly Planner to schedule each item that corresponds with the explanations.

The following pages explain each activity in detail and list the individuals on the team that are responsible fo the completion of each item. The Team Coordinator does not always participate in each activity. However, he/she is responsible for the training, coordination, follow-up and completion of each item. At the end of the Team Coordinator Section is the Planning Calendar so that he/she can assign and control each activity.

OTHER TEAM MEMBERS
CEO
VP Marketing
VP Accounting
Area Sales Managers
Account Executives
Technology Manager

Step 1. Hold pre-event planning meeting with key management.

Discuss:
Dates and times
Who will manage?
Who will assist?
Create client company guidelines on which companies to invite
Prepare preliminary schedule of events and activities

HOSPITALITY EVENT PLANNING CALENDAR

WEEK	DUTY	COORDINATOR	DATE FINISHED
4	ATTEND MEETING TO REVIEW SCHEDULE AND TEAM MEMBER RESPONSIBILITIES – CONDUCTED BY TEAM COORDINATOR	ALL TEAM MEMBERS	
4	BEGIN DAILY DIARY OF ACTIVITIES.ON A DAILY BASIS DOCUMENT THE ACTIVITIES AND THEIR COMPLETION.	TEAM COORDINATOR	
4	ADEQUATE SUPPLIES SHOULD BE ORDERED FOR THE CUSTOMER APPRECIATION DAY. QUANTITIES TO BE DETERMINED BY TEAM COORD AND FIELD COORDINATOR.	FIELD COORDINATOR	
4	ALL BIDS FOR WORK TO BE COMPLETED BY OUTSIDE VENDORS COMPLETED AND SENT FOR APPROVAL OF APPROPRIATE MANAGEMENT INDIVIDUALS.	TEAM COORDINATOR, FIELD COORDINATOR	
4	PLACE ALL EQUIPMENT ORDERS. OBTAIN ARRIVAL DATES TO ENSURE THEY ARRIVE ON TIME	TEAM COORDINATOR, FIELD COORDINATOR	
4	OBTAIN NAMES OF ALL EVENT PERSONNEL FROM MANAGEMENT AND ARRANGE FOR TRAINING CLASS	FIELD COORDINATOR	
4	PURSUE AVAILABILITY OF GOLF CART	FIELD COORDINATOR	

	RENTAL AND EVENT CREDENTIALS		
4	WRITE INVITATIONS, LETTERS, MAPS, INSTRUCTIONS TO CUSTOMERS	TEAM COORDINATOR, FIELD COORDINATOR	
4	CONTACT EVENT OFFICIALS ON GETTING NECESSARY TICKETS, OTHER ARRANGEMENTS, ETC.	TEAM COORDINATOR	
4	PREPARE MOCK UPS AND PRINT ANY ANNOUNCEMENTS AND ADVERTISING BROCHURES, MAPS, ETC.	TEAM COORDINATOR	
4	DISCUSS INVITEE GUIDELINES AND SET DEADLINE FOR RECEIVING LIST OF INVITEES FROM ACCOUNT EXECUTIVES	TEAM COORDINATOR VP MARKETING ACCOUNT EXECUTIVES	
4	FINALIZE EVENT ACTIVITIES AND SCHEDULE TIMES FOR ALL ACTIVITIES	TEAM COORDINATOR VP MARKETING ACCOUNT EXECUTIVES	
3	TRAINING CLASS FOR EVENT PERSONNEL TRAINING AND RESPONSIBILITIES -SET-UP -SALES ACTIVITIES -WRAP-UP -SUPPLIES -WORK SCHEDULE	TEAM COORDINATOR, FIELD COORDINATOR	
3	IDENTIFY SALES TEAM LEADER(SALES ASSOC 1)	TEAM COORDINATOR, VP MARKETING	
3	DESIGN WELCOMING COUNTER SETUP	TEAM COORDINATOR, SALES ASSOC 1	
3	DETERMINE POWER SUPPLY AND COMMUNICATION	TEAM COORDINATOR,	

	NEEDS, ORDER PHONES, LAPTOPS, CELL PHONES, WALKIE-TALKIES, PAGERS, ETC.	FIELD COORDINATOR, SALES ASSOC 1 TECHNOLOGY MANAGER	
3	FINALIZE HOSPITALITY ARRANGEMENTS WITH SUBCONTRACTORS, GET FINAL WRITTEN CONFIRMATION OF COSTS AND FINALIZE SCHEDULE	TEAM COORDINATOR, FIELD COORDINATOR, VP ACCOUNTING	
3	OBTAIN ALL COMMUNICATION DEVICES/SET UP TEXT GROUP FOR CELL PHONE COMMUNICATION (MAKE SURE YOU DON'T LEAVE SOMEONE OUT)	FIELD COORDINATOR	
3	DEVELOP DISPLAYS, BANNERS, GIVEAWAYS, AND OTHER ATTENTION-GETTING DEVICES TO BE USED -CONTACT ALL SUPPLIERS, GET PRICES -PLACE ORDERS	TEAM COORDINATOR, FIELD COORDINATOR, SALES ASSOC 1	
3	ARRANGE FOR ASSISTANCE RE: PHOTOGRAPHS, ARTICLES, ETC.	FIELD COORDINATOR, SALES ASSOC 1	
3	FINALIZE LIST OF INVITEES – HOLD CONFERENCE CALL PREPARE ALPHABETICAL LIST BY COMPANY NAME PREPARE ALPHABETICAL LIST BY INDIVIDUAL FIRST NAME	FIELD COORDINATOR, VP MARKETING, AREA SALES MANAGERS, ACCOUNT EXECUTIVES	

	PREPARE ALPHABETICAL LIST BY INDIVIDUAL LAST NAME DISTRIBUTE ABOVE TO ALL TEAM MEMBERS		
3	PREPARE THANK YOU LETTERS, PRINT AND SCHEDULE MAILING AFTER THE EVENT	TEAM COORDINATOR	
2	FINALIZE TENT LAYOUT, MAKE SURE ALL ARRANGEMENTS HAVE BEEN MADE. OBTAIN TENT LAYOUT DRAWING.	FIELD COORDINATOR, FIELD COORDINATOR, SALES ASSOC 1	
2	FOLLOW UP ON ALL EQUIPMENT NEEDS	FIELD COORDINATOR	
2	FOLLOW UP ON ALL SUPPLY ORDERS	FIELD COORDINATOR	
2	FOLLOW UP ON ALL COMMUNICATION DEVICES – IS EVERYONE CONNECTED AND GETTING MESSAGES?	FIELD COORDINATOR	
2	TEST COMPUTER NETWORKS, WIRELESS CONNECTIONS, ETC. MAKE SURE THE VENUE HAS AN ADEQUATE WIRELESS HOTSPOT	FIELD COORDINATOR, TECHNOLOGY MANAGER	
2	DEFINE OPERATING PLAN FOR THE EVENT – SCHEDULE WALK THROUGH OF THE FACILITY AND/OR TENT	TEAM COORDINATOR, FIELD COORDINATOR, SALES ASSOC 1	
1	FOLLOW UP ON ALL EQUIPMENT ORDERS – REPORT STATUS TO TEAM COORDINATOR DISCUSS: -COMMUNICATIONS PLANS	TEAM COORDINATOR, FIELD COORDINATOR, SALES ASSOC 1	

	-LAPTOP PLAN -SIGNS/DISPLAYS, ETC. -SUPPLY ORDERS AND DELIVERY DATES -OTHER EQUIPMENT		
1	PREPARE AND TEST ALL EQUIPMENT DURING WALK THROUGH	TEAM	
1	MONDAY TEAM REVIEW MTG. REVIEW STATUS OF SCHEDULE, PLAN TO FINISH INCOMPLETE TASKS BY THURSDAY THIS WEEK	TEAM	
1	PLAN ON BEING AVAILABLE ALL WEEK FOR ANY LAST MINUTE PREPARATION	TEAM	
1	THURSDAY, REVIEW SCHEDULE AND OPERATING PLAN	TEAM	
1	OBTAIN ALL CLEANING MATERIALS	SALES ASSOC 1	
1	INSPECT TENT AND SETUP, CLEAN AND ORGANIZED BEFORE LEAVING, FIRST IMPRESSION VERY IMPORTANT	VP MARKETING, TEAM COORDINATOR, FIELD COORDINATOR, SALES ASSOC 1	
1	TEST ALL EQUIPMENT	FIELD COORDINATOR, SALES ASSOC 1	
1	FINISH ALL INCOMPLETE TASKS	TEAM	
1	OBTAIN PETTY CASH FOR ANY UNEXPECTED CONTINGENCIES	FIELD COORDINATOR	
1	FINALIZE POST-EVENT REPORTING PROCEDURES AND ITEMS THAT WILL BE KEPT TRACK OF NUMERICALLY	FIELD COORDINATOR SALES ASSOC 1	

0	ALL TEAM MEMBER NEED TO BE PRESENT ON DAY 1 TO ENSURE SMOOTH OPERATION	ALL TEAM MEMBERS	
0	DAILY REVIEW MEETING. ANY PROBLEMS MUST BE REVIEWED AND A PLAN MADE TO CORRECT BEFORE THE NEXT DAY.	ALL TEAM MEMBERS	
0	POST-EVENT – WRITE FINAL REPORT – WHAT WENT RIGHT, WHAT WENT WRONG	TEAM COORDINATOR	
0	FINALIZE/EDIT HANDBOOK – PREPARE FOR NEXT YEAR	TEAM COORDINATOR	

Supplement to Planning Calendar

WEEK	ACTIVITY	TEAM MEMBERS	DATE FINISHED

CUSTOMER APPRECIATION DAY Sample Final Report

ON MAY 8 AND 15, INDIANA DISTRICT HELD ITS ANNUAL CUSTOMER APPRECIATION DAY ACTIVITIES AT THE INDIANAPOLIS MOTOR SPEEDWAY. ON MAY 3, ABOUT 40 CUSTOMERS VISITED THE "TURN TWO" SUITE. THE DAY WAS A SUCCESS AS FORECASTED RAIN HELD OFF AND CUSTOMERS SAW EXCITING INDY CAR PRACTICE (IN PREPARATION FOR THE INDIANAPOLIS 500 MILE RACE). MAY 15 SAW OVER 420 PEOPLE VISIT OUR TENT AND SUITES. ALL CUSTOMERS WERE TREATED TO PIT AND GARAGE TOURS AND MANY SPENT TIME IN OUR TURN TWO SUITE. OVER 130 COMPANIES WERE REPRESENTED. VOLUME FIGURES WITH THESE CUSTOMERS (MAY 2005 VS. MAY 2006) SHOWED A 57 % INCREASE IN TOTAL VOLUME FROM 101,288 AVERAGE WEEKLY PACKAGES TO 159,477.

CUSTOMER APPRECIATION DAY HOSPITALITY ISSUES:

WHAT WENT RIGHT
-WEATHER ON BOTH DAYS WAS EXCEPTIONALLY GOOD. THIS MADE FOR AN OVERALL PLEASANT ATMOSPHERE FOR OUR CUSTOMERS.
-CUSTOMER SERVICE PEOPLE WERE EXTREMELY HELPFUL AND WILLING TO ASSIST IN ANY LAST MINUTE DETAIL. SEVERAL PEOPLE CAME EARLY AND ASSISTED WITH SET UP ARRANGEMENTS AND GREETING EARLY-ARRIVING CUSTOMERS. TOURS AND DIRECTIONS FOR CUSTOMERS WERE ABLY HANDLED AS WELL.
-HAVING THE SUITE AVAILABLE ONLY TO OUR MAJOR CUSTOMERS ON MAY 8 PROVED VERY SUCCESSFUL. THESE CUSTOMERS RECEIVED FIRST CLASS TREATMENT AND HAD A QUALITY TIME. BEING ABLE TO ENJOY THE SUITE ENVIRONMENT WITHOUT CROWDING WAS A PLUS.
-ONE GUEST WAS ABLE TO REKINDLE A FRIENDSHIP WITH AN INDY CAR DRIVER WHOM HE HAD KNOWN IN MEXICO. THIS WAS A SPECIAL TREAT FOR HIM AS HE WAS NOT AWARE THAT THIS PERSON WAS NOW DRIVING INDY CARS.
-MANY CUSTOMERS WERE THRILLED TO SEE MARIO ANDRETTI STANDING ON THE BALCONY OF THE SUITE NEXT TO OURS. HE WAS THERE FOR OVER AN HOUR AND PROVIDED A GREAT PHOTO OPPORTUNITY FOR OUR CUSTOMERS.
-PIT AND GARAGE TOURS WERE HANDLED WELL. A SHUTTLE CAME BY REGULARLY TO PROVIDE TRANSPORTATION BETWEEN TURN TWO AND THE GARAGE AREA.
-IMS OFFICIALS WERE EXTREMELY HELPFUL AND COURTEOUS. THEY MADE THE DAY EASIER FOR ALL CONCERNED.
-THE USE OF A RENTED TENT ON THE 15TH PROVIDED PLENTY OF SPACE FOR OUR CUSTOMERS AND A RELAXED ATMOSPHERE. THERE WAS PLENTY OF OPPORTUNITY FOR QUALITY TIME WITH OUR CUSTOMERS.

-ACCOUNT EXECUTIVES AND AREA MANAGERS DID AN EXCELLENT JOB OF DISTRIBUTING TICKETS AND INVITATIONS. VERY FEW LAST MINUTE CHANGES WERE MADE AND THE WHOLE EVENT LOOKED ORGANIZED AND CONTROLLED.

-VISITS TO THE TENT BY INDY CAR DRIVERS PROVIDED AN EXTRA TREAT FOR OUR CUSTOMERS. THE PHOTO OPPORTUNITIES THEY PROVIDED WERE A THRILL FOR OUR CUSTOMERS.

-EXPENDITURES WERE KEPT TO A MINIMUM COMPARED TO THE LAST FEW YEARS.

-REQUIRING LOCAL CUSTOMERS TO FIND THEIR WAY TO THE TRACK REDUCED EXPENDITURES AND THE NUMBER OF COMPANY PEOPLE REQUIRED FOP SPECIAL DUTIES AND DRIVING.

-THE AVAILABILITY OF BEER ONLY (NOT MIXED-DRINKS) IN THE TENT AND SUITE REDUCED THE AMOUNT OF DRINKING OUR CUSTOMERS ENGAGED IN. THIS HELPED CREATE A SITUATION WHERE THERE WERE NO NOTICEABLY DRUNK OR UNRULY CUSTOMERS WHICH MADE THE DAY MORE PLEASANT FOR OTHER CUSTOMERS AND COMPANY EMPLOYEES.

-NAMETAGS PROVIDED FOR OUR CUSTOMERS LOOKED MORE ATTRACTIVE AND PROFESSIONAL THAN TAGS OF OTHER COMPANIES AT THE SPEEDWAY.

-MOST ACTIVITIES REQUIRED TO MAKE THESE DAYS A SUCCESS WERE PROPERLY ASSIGNED AND COORDINATED SO THAT FEW LOOSE ENDS REMAINED WHEN CUSTOMER APPRECIATION DAYS ARRIVED.

WHAT WENT WRONG
-AN ALPHABETICALLY SORTED LIST OF CUSTOMERS SHOULD HAVE BEEN AVAILABLE AT THE TENT IN ORDER TO PROPERLY RECORD ARRIVING GUESTS. FOR THE FIRST FEW MINUTES AS CUSTOMERS ARRIVED, THE ENTRANCE TO THE TENT WAS CROWDED AND SEEMED DISORGANIZED.

-PRE-ASSIGNED RESPONSIBILITIES SHOULD HAVE BEEN GIVEN TO VARIOUS CUSTOMER SERVICE PEOPLE FOR SUCH ACTIVITIES AS GREETER, TOUR GUIDE, TOUR COORDINATOR, NAME BADGE ISSUER, ETC. AS IT WAS, THESE POSITIONS WERE NOT ASSIGNED UNTIL A NEED WAS DETERMINED. THIS SITUATION WAS CREATED BECAUSE MANY OF OUR CUSTOMERS ARRIVED EARLY. THIS WAS UNANTICIPATED IN THIS OUR FIRST TENT PARTY.

-MANY GARAGE PASS TICKETS WENT UNUSED AS OUR CUSTOMERS DID NOT FIND THIS TOUR AS APPEALING AS A WALK THROUGH THE PITS OR A TRIP TO THE SUITE.

-PIT AND SUITE PASS PROCEDURES SHOULD HAVE INCLUDED A CONTROL SHEET. AS IT WAS, WE WROTE NAMES ON 8 1/2" NOTEBOOK PAPER. THIS LOOKED UNPROFESSIONAL.

-ALTHOUGH SOME CUSTOMERS APPRECIATED BEING ABLE TO TAKE POLAROIDS (THAT WE PROVIDED) AND HAVE THESE AS SOUVENIRS, FEW CUSTOMERS AVAILED THEMSELVES OF IT,

Sample Client Thank You Letter

Dear _____

Thanks for accepting our invitation to join us at the Indianapolis Motor Speedway for Customer Appreciation Day on May 8th. I look forward to spending an enjoyable day with you.

Enclosed you will find a map of the Speedway grounds. Please use this map to find the location of our suite, suggested parking areas, and best entrance point at the track. Also find your suite tickets. Our Suite number is 174.

If you would like to tour Gasoline Alley or the pit area, be advised that the Speedway does maintain a dress standard. Please do not wear shorts (or skirts) whose hems are higher than two inches above the knee. Also, no open-toed sandals or sleeveless shirts should be worn. These regulations are strictly enforced by Speedway personnel. Also, please bring your driver's license as it will be needed for admittance to these areas.

The Corporate suite is scheduled to open at 10:00 AM. Thanks again for joining us.

Sincerely,

Robert Villegas
Hospitality Coordinator

Sample Facility Map

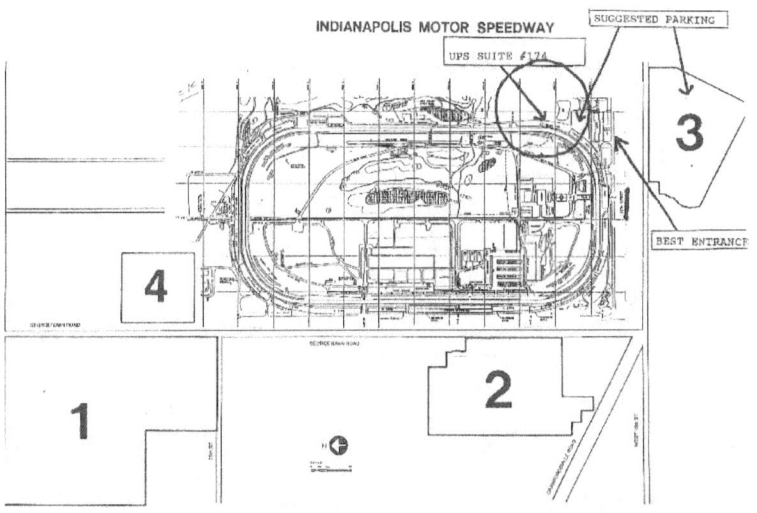

INDIANAPOLIS MOTOR SPEEDWAY

UPS SUITE #174

SUGGESTED PARKING

3

BEST ENTRANCE

4

1

2

Sample Directions Map

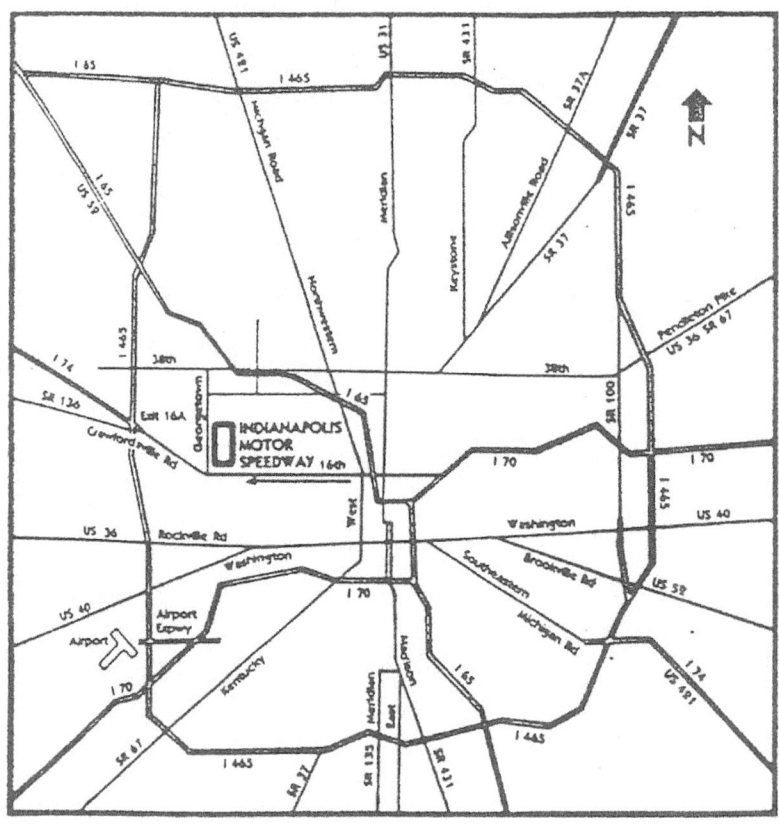

*I-465, North/South Leg, Exit 16A

BLANK IMPLEMENTATION PLANNING CALENDAR

WEEK	ACTIVITY	TEAM MEMBERS	DATE FINISHED

WEEK	ACTIVITY	TEAM MEMBERS	DATE FINISHED

WEEK	ACTIVITY	TEAM MEMBERS	DATE FINISHED

WEEK	ACTIVITY	TEAM MEMBERS	DATE FINISHED

NOTES

www.ingramcontent.com/pod-product-compliance
Lightning Source LLC
Chambersburg PA
CBHW070929180526
45168CB00005B/2205